MAKER MODELS
CASTLE

Anna Claybourne

WAYLAND
www.waylandbooks.co.uk

First published in Great Britain in 2019
by Wayland
Copyright © Hodder and Stoughton, 2019
All rights reserved

Editor: Elise Short
Design and illustration: Collaborate

HB ISBN 978 1 5263 0749 1
PB ISBN 978 1 5263 0750 7

Printed and bound in China

Wayland, an imprint of
Hachette Children's Group
Part of Hodder and Stoughton
Carmelite House
50 Victoria Embankment
London EC4Y 0DZ

An Hachette UK Company

www.hachette.co.uk
www.hachettechildrens.co.uk

CONTENTS

HOLDING THE FORT

Since ancient times, people have built castles and forts: big stone buildings designed to guard the land around them and keep enemies out. They were often homes, too, for kings, queens, lords and ladies, and knights – armoured soldiers on horseback.

If you love castles, knights and fairytales, this book is for you. It shows you how to build your own castle, complete with a working door, portcullis and drawbridge, a moat, turrets and waving flags. There's also a tilt yard for jousting knights and a mangonel for battles – all made from cardboard boxes, craft materials and other everyday items.

MAKE IT YOUR OWN!

The castle in this book is a traditional stone castle from medieval times, but you don't have to make yours exactly the same if you don't want to. Let your imagination go wild and create the castle of your dreams. Maybe you could recreate a castle from your favourite book or film. It's up to you!

MAKER MATERIALS

The projects in this book have been designed to work using things you can find at home, such as disposable containers, packaging and basic art and craft equipment. If you don't have what you need, you can usually get it at a hobby or craft shop, supermarket or DIY store, or by ordering online. See page 31 for a list of useful sources.

TIP

Charity shops are a great place to look for old, cheap household items and materials, too.

BLOOP BLOOP! SAFETY ALERT!

For some of the projects you'll need to use sharp tools, such as a craft knife or a bradawl (a pointed tool for making holes). You might also want to use an electric appliance such as a hot glue gun.

For anything involving sharp objects, heat or electricity, always ask an adult to help and supervise. Make sure you keep items like these in a safe place, away from where younger children could find them.

CAN I USE THIS?

Before you start emptying the cupboards, make sure any containers or other household items you want to use are finished with, clean and you have permission to take them for your creations. Let the castle-making commence!

CASTLE WALLS AND BATTLEMENTS

Start by making the basic structure of your castle – the walls and battlements – from a cardboard box. It can be any size, but a medium-sized box will be easiest to work with.

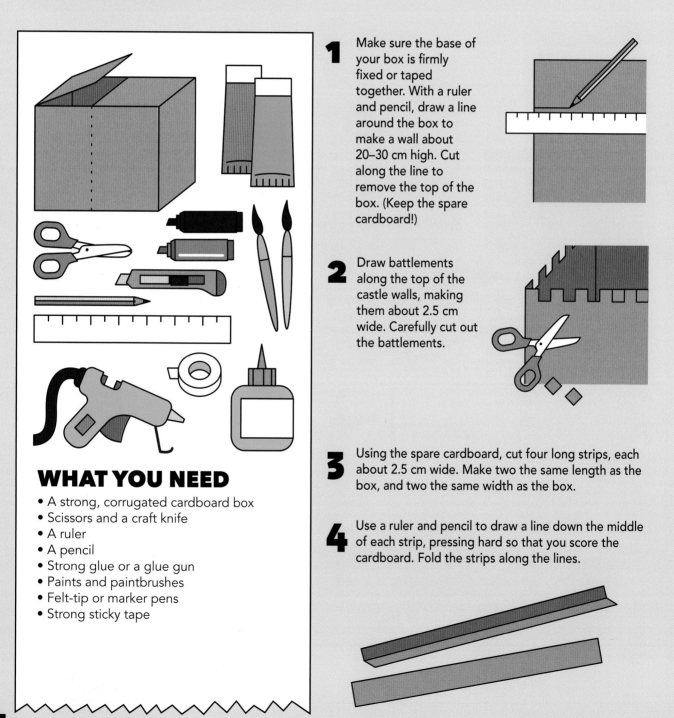

WHAT YOU NEED

- A strong, corrugated cardboard box
- Scissors and a craft knife
- A ruler
- A pencil
- Strong glue or a glue gun
- Paints and paintbrushes
- Felt-tip or marker pens
- Strong sticky tape

1 Make sure the base of your box is firmly fixed or taped together. With a ruler and pencil, draw a line around the box to make a wall about 20–30 cm high. Cut along the line to remove the top of the box. (Keep the spare cardboard!)

2 Draw battlements along the top of the castle walls, making them about 2.5 cm wide. Carefully cut out the battlements.

3 Using the spare cardboard, cut four long strips, each about 2.5 cm wide. Make two the same length as the box, and two the same width as the box.

4 Use a ruler and pencil to draw a line down the middle of each strip, pressing hard so that you score the cardboard. Fold the strips along the lines.

5 Fit the strips inside the castle just below the battlements, making them overlap at the corners. Glue them in place. These are the walkways that allow guards to stand on the battlements.

6 Cut another long strip of card about 2 cm wide, and make a fold every 1 cm, folding first one way then the other to make steps. Fold small strips of cardboard (1 cm wide, 2 cm long) in half to make tabs. Use these to glue the steps to the inside of one wall, leading up to the walkway.

7 To decorate your castle, paint the walls all over. Once it's dry, draw stonework.

THE HISTORY BIT!

Long ago, kings, queens, lords, ladies and knights had castles to live in, and to control the surrounding area. During wars and battles, people would take refuge in them, so castles had to be strong and well defended.

TIP

Our castle is open at the top and has no roof, so you can see and reach inside easily. If you want a roof, build the rest of the castle first, then make a simple roof from another piece of card.

TAKE IT FURTHER ...

For a bigger, more complicated castle, you can prepare more boxes in the same way and glue them to the first one.

TOWERS AND TURRETS

Your castle isn't looking very castle-like yet … because it needs towers and turrets! They're easy to make from cardboard tubes.

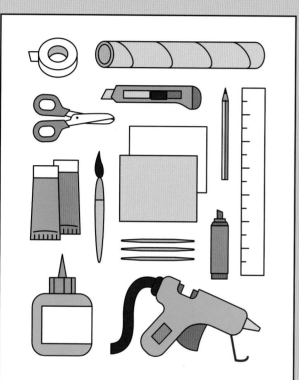

WHAT YOU NEED

- Four strong, wide cardboard tubes, such as poster tubes or snack or crisps tubes
- Scissors and a craft knife
- A pencil and a ruler
- Card
- Strong glue or a glue gun
- Sticky tape (invisible if possible)
- Wooden skewers or cocktail sticks
- Paper
- Felt-tip or marker pens
- Paints and paintbrushes

Kitchen roll tubes will work too, but they will make narrower towers and won't be quite as strong.

1 Cut your tubes to a good height for your towers – about 10 cm taller than your castle walls. If you're using long poster tubes, you may be able to cut two or more castle towers from each one.

2 Hold one tube against your castle walls and mark the height of the wall all around your tube. Turn the tube upside down and mark its base into quarters. Pick one quarter of the tube and draw lines from two marks next to each other up the sides of your tube all the way up to the line marking the height of your castle walls.

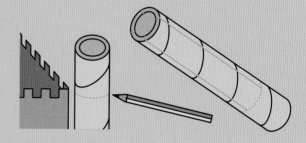

3 Carefully cut out this shape with scissors or a craft knife. Repeat steps 2 and 3 for the other tubes. You should now be able to fit the towers to the corners of the castle.

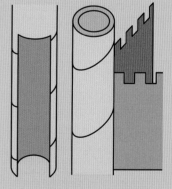

4 Mark battlements around the top of the tubes and cut them out. You can also mark windows or arrow slits on the towers and cut these out too.

5 On a piece of card, draw four circles by drawing around the end of a tower. Draw a 1 cm border around each circle. Cut them out. Cut slits into the edges to make tabs, and fold them down. Glue the circles inside the top of the towers, below the battlements.

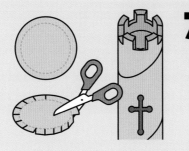

6 Now draw two bigger circles, twice the width of the towers, on card. Draw a 1 cm border around both circles and cut them out. Cut each circle in half. Cut into the curved edges to make tabs. Curve each piece around to make a pointed turret roof that will fit inside the towers, and tape each roof together.

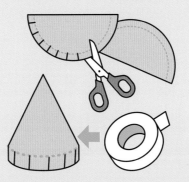

7 Fold in the tabs and glue the pointed roofs on to the card inside the tops of the towers. Make flags using wooden skewers or cocktail sticks. Glue a piece of folded paper to the top of each stick. Decorate the flags and push the flagpoles into the top of each turret.

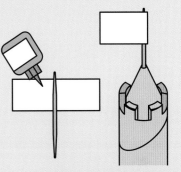

8 If you like, paint or decorate the towers. When they are dry, fit them on to the corners of the castle. Use glue to hold them in place.

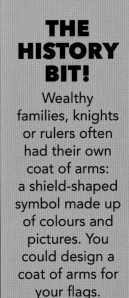

THE HISTORY BIT!
Wealthy families, knights or rulers often had their own coat of arms: a shield-shaped symbol made up of colours and pictures. You could design a coat of arms for your flags.

THE GRAND GATEHOUSE

At the front of every good castle is the gatehouse, a grand entrance with its own mini-turrets.

WHAT YOU NEED

- Two flattish cardboard boxes, one larger, one smaller
- Two cardboard tubes (kitchen roll tubes are perfect)
- Scissors and a craft knife
- A pencil and a ruler
- Card
- Strong glue or a glue gun
- Wooden skewers or cocktail sticks
- Paper
- Felt-tip or marker pens
- Paints and paintbrushes

The larger box should be thinner than your cardboard tubes, but taller than the height of the castle walls. Chocolate boxes are a good option. The smaller box should be a similar width to the larger box, but shorter and thinner.

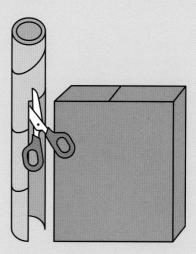

1 Hold the side of the larger box against one of the cardboard tubes. Draw around it on to the tube. Cut out the shape so that the tube can slot on to the side of the box. Do the same with the other tube.

2 Draw small battlements around the tops of the two tubes and cut them out. You can also make turret roofs and flags, as shown on pages 8–9, or if you prefer, just leave them as they are.

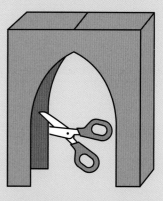

3 Draw an arched or rounded doorway on the front and centre of the larger box. Cut out the doorway from both the front and the back of the box.

4 Cut a long strip of card (the length of the outline of the archway) to fit in the gap between the front and back of the archway with an extra 1 cm along each side. Cut slots into the edge to make tabs. Carefully glue this strip along the inside edge of the doorway.

Glue the towers in place on the sides of the box. Then take the smaller box and stand the gatehouse on top of it. Glue the gatehouse on to it.

Once the glue is dry, stand the gatehouse up against the front of the castle, and mark lines on the castle walls about 1 cm in from each edge of the gatehouse towers. Carefully cut out and remove the section from the front of the castle between the two marks.

Cut slots in the outside edges of the gatehouse, through the tubes and the smaller box, so that you can slot it on to the castle walls.

1 cm

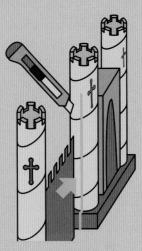

If you need to, trim a small amount off the ends of the walkway to get a good fit. Once you're happy with the position of the gatehouse, glue it in place.

Finally, if you like, paint the gatehouse and draw patterns to look like stonework.

11

DOOR AND PORTCULLIS

No castle is complete without a sturdy wooden door and an iron portcullis for extra protection against invaders.

1 On the corrugated card, draw a door shape that will fit loosely inside the archway of your gatehouse. Cut it out. Draw around it to make a second, matching door.

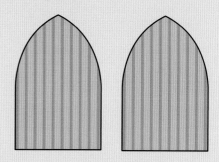

2 Cut four small pieces of smooth card, about 1 cm wide by 3 cm long. Fold them in half. Glue two on each side of one of the door shapes and make sure the folded edges stick out a little.

3 Glue the second door shape on top of the first, so that the cardboard tabs are sandwiched in between them and the folds stick out at the sides to make hinges. If you like, paint or colour in the door.

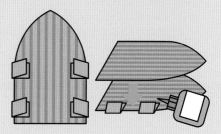

4 Measure the length between the two hinges on each side of the door. Cut two pieces of straw just slightly shorter than this length.

5 Now measure the length between the upper and lower edges of the hinges. Cut two pieces of wooden skewer or cocktail stick slightly longer than this length.

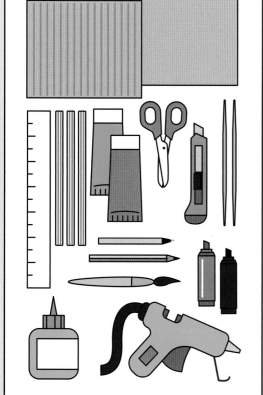

WHAT YOU NEED

- Thick corrugated card
- Thinner smooth card
- Scissors and a craft knife
- A pencil and a ruler
- Strong glue or a glue gun
- Wooden skewers or cocktail sticks
- Three non-bendy paper or plastic straws
- Paints and paintbrushes
- Felt-tip or marker pens
- Silver paint or pen

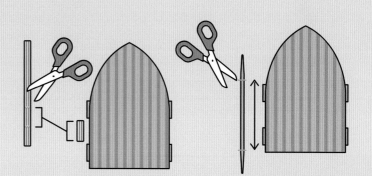

6 Fit the straws in the gaps between the hinges and push the skewers through the hinges and through the straws in between them. The hinges should hold the skewers tightly, but if they don't, add a bit of glue. (DON'T get glue on the straw!)

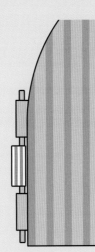

7 Carefully cut the door in half, up the middle, to make two doors. Check they fit inside the gatehouse – if they don't, trim a little off the middle edge of each door.

8 Use strong glue to fix the straws to the insides of the gatehouse doorway, so that the doors meet in the middle. When the glue is dry, you should be able to open and close the doors.

PORTCULLIS

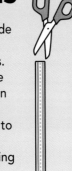

1 Cut along one side of the two remaining straws. Position and glue the two straws on the sides of the gatehouse, next to the towers, with the cut sides facing each other.

2 Measure the width between the outer edges of the straws. On smooth card, draw a portcullis the same width across. Cut it out and colour or paint it silver (or grey if you don't have silver). When it's dry, slot it between the straws, so it can slide up and down.

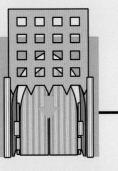

TIP

If you have silver-coloured card, it will make a great portcullis. You can sometimes find it in packaging, or in a hobby store.

RAISE THE DRAWBRIDGE!

For extra security, many castles had a moat around them, with a drawbridge across it. The drawbridge could be raised so that enemies couldn't get across the water.

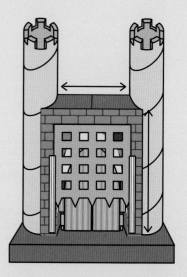

1 Measure the width between the gatehouse towers and the height of the middle of the gatehouse. On the thick corrugated cardboard, draw a rectangle with this width and height. Cut it out.

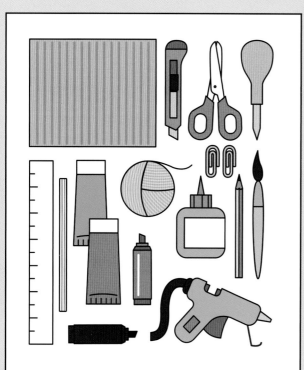

WHAT YOU NEED

- Thick corrugated card
- A non-bendy straw
- Scissors and a craft knife
- A pencil and a ruler
- Strong glue or a glue gun
- Thick string
- A bradawl or large needle
- Paints and paintbrushes
- Felt-tip or marker pens
- Two metal paper clips

A straw should work for this, but if it's not long enough, try using a long chopstick or skewer instead.

2 Use a bradawl or large needle to make four small holes in the corners of the rectangle. You can then paint or colour it to look like wooden planks.

3 Take the two paper clips, unfold them and bend them into long U-shapes. Loop them into the holes in one end of the drawbridge, then push the ends into the base of the gatehouse, between the towers. (If it's hard to get them in, make small holes first.)

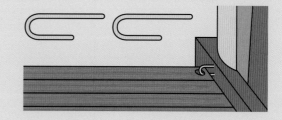

4 Use a bit of glue to stick the paper clips in place, with the loops sticking out a little way so that the drawbridge can move freely up and down.

5 Cut two pieces of string, each about 50 cm long. Tie the ends of the strings into the two holes at the other end of the drawbridge.

6 Mark dots on the sides of both of the gatehouse towers, using a ruler to make sure they are all at the same level. Use a sharp pencil to make holes just big enough for the straw to fit through tightly.

7 Push the straw through all the holes. Take the loose ends of the two strings and tie them around the middle of the straw. Glue them down as well, so that the string can't slip around the straw.

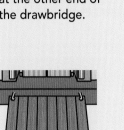

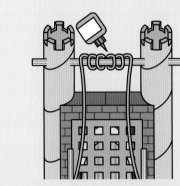

8 When the glue is dry, turn the straw round and round so that the string winds around it, pulling the drawbridge up. To lower the drawbridge, turn the straw the other way!

THE HISTORY BIT!

Invading a castle with a raised drawbridge was tough. Guards would fire arrows at attackers from the top of the gatehouse. The raised drawbridge and the portcullis both protected the doorway, but if anyone did get in, the guards dropped rocks, hot oil or boiling water on them. Ouch!

THE GREAT HALL

The great hall is the biggest room in the castle, where feasts and dances are held. It has dining tables and benches, lit by candlelight.

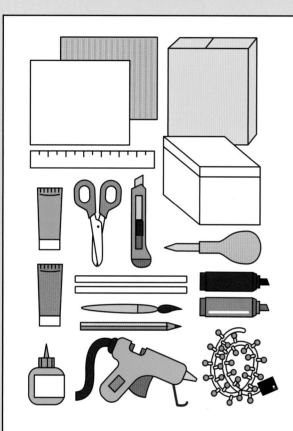

WHAT YOU NEED

- A strong cardboard box, such as a shoebox
- Paper
- Scissors and a craft knife
- A pencil and a ruler
- Paints and paintbrushes
- Felt-tip or marker pens
- Thick corrugated card
- Strong glue or a glue gun
- A flat wide cardboard box
- Sticky tape
- Bradawl or large needle
- Small battery-powered fairy lights (optional)
- White straws (optional)

1 Measure the inside of the castle from front to back and one-third of the distance across it. Mark these measurements on the underneath of your shoebox. Cut this shape out and fit it inside the castle to make a room on one side.

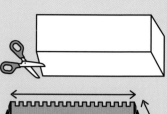

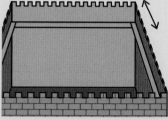

2 The remaining space is your great hall. Measure its length and width and cut out a piece of paper the right size to fit in it. Paint or draw floorboards or floor tiles on the paper. When it's dry, glue it to the floor of the main hall.

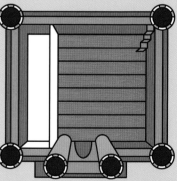

3 If you like, you can decorate the walls inside the hall with medieval tapestry wall hangings. Draw them on pieces of paper and colour them in, then glue them to the walls.

4 To make a dining table, cut a long rectangle from thick corrugated card, a thinner strip of card the same length and two small shapes. Fold the small shapes in half and glue them to the table to make legs. Cut slots in the legs. Fit the card strip into them.

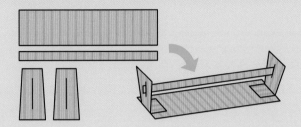

5 You can make benches the same way – just make them lower and thinner. Make two benches for each table and arrange them around the hall.

6 To make a row of candles, cut the end off the wide flat box to make a long shallow tray shape. Make a row of holes along one side.

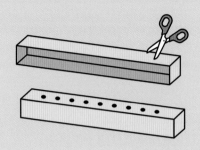

7 If you have a set of fairy lights, make a hole in the castle's back wall, and thread the string of lights through it. Leave the battery hidden behind the castle. Poke a light through each hole in the tray, so it sticks up like a candle. Tape down the wire inside the tray.

8 Glue the tray to the wall over the hole you made, with the lights sticking up and switch them on. Or, if you don't have fairy lights, stick model candles along the tray, made of short pieces of a white straw with a coloured paper flame on top.

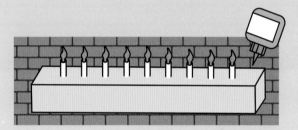

TAKE IT FURTHER ...

What else could you add? Try designing and making a fireplace, a throne, or even tiny plates, goblets and food.

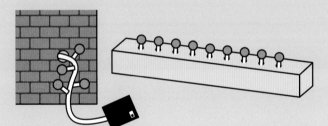

TIP

If you have model figures or knights to put in your castle, make the tables and benches the right size for them to use.

THE BEDCHAMBER

The lord or lady of a castle had their own fancy bedchamber, complete with a four-poster bed and a close-stool. What was a close-stool? A type of toilet that looked like a chair!

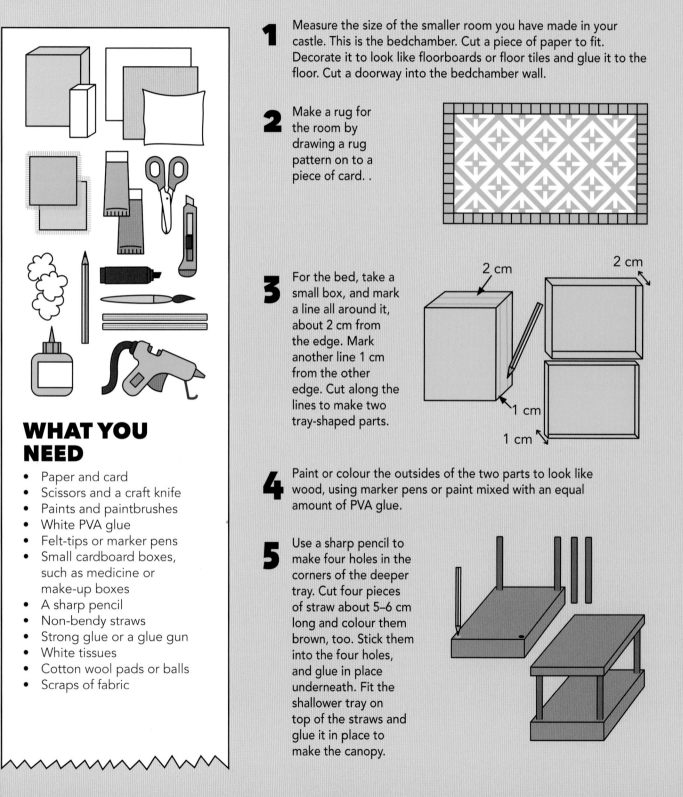

1 Measure the size of the smaller room you have made in your castle. This is the bedchamber. Cut a piece of paper to fit. Decorate it to look like floorboards or floor tiles and glue it to the floor. Cut a doorway into the bedchamber wall.

2 Make a rug for the room by drawing a rug pattern on to a piece of card. .

3 For the bed, take a small box, and mark a line all around it, about 2 cm from the edge. Mark another line 1 cm from the other edge. Cut along the lines to make two tray-shaped parts.

2 cm
2 cm
1 cm
1 cm

4 Paint or colour the outsides of the two parts to look like wood, using marker pens or paint mixed with an equal amount of PVA glue.

5 Use a sharp pencil to make four holes in the corners of the deeper tray. Cut four pieces of straw about 5–6 cm long and colour them brown, too. Stick them into the four holes, and glue in place underneath. Fit the shallower tray on top of the straws and glue it in place to make the canopy.

WHAT YOU NEED

- Paper and card
- Scissors and a craft knife
- Paints and paintbrushes
- White PVA glue
- Felt-tips or marker pens
- Small cardboard boxes, such as medicine or make-up boxes
- A sharp pencil
- Non-bendy straws
- Strong glue or a glue gun
- White tissues
- Cotton wool pads or balls
- Scraps of fabric

6 To make a pillow, fold a tissue around some cotton wool and glue it down. Use pieces of fabric to make bedcovers.

7 For the close-stool, cut a piece off the end of a small, long box, such as a lipstick box. Cut a round hole in the top. Cut the flap from the other end of the box and glue it to the side of the stool to make a seat cover.

8 Cut a longer rectangle of card and stick it to the back of the stool, over where the flap is stuck on. Finally, paint or decorate the close-stool.

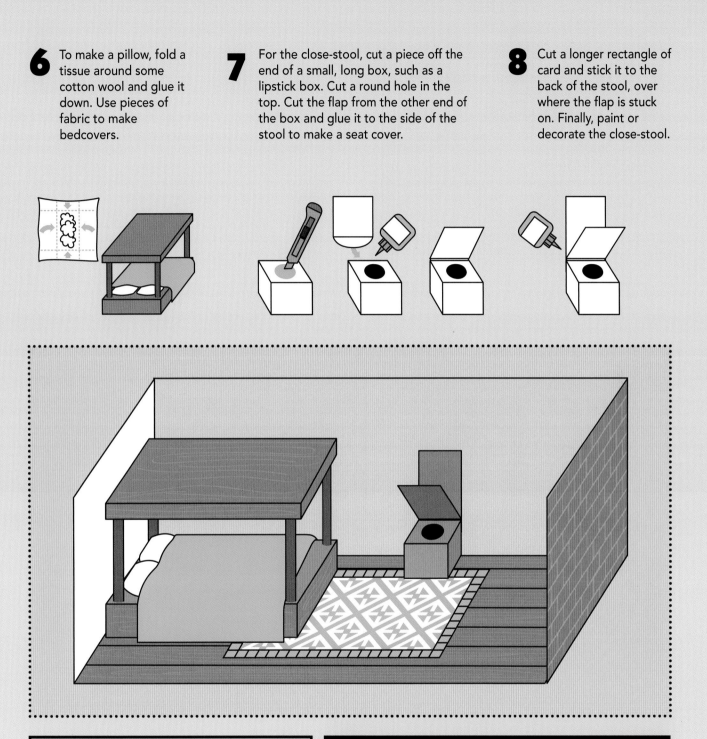

THE HISTORY BIT!

In medieval times, castles didn't have proper flushing toilets. A bowl inside the close-stool collected the poo and wee, and an unlucky servant would have to empty it!

TAKE IT FURTHER ...

What else could you design and make for the bedchamber? What about wood panelling for the walls, or a portrait painting? The lord or lady might also like a candlestick, a pet dog or a tiny book to read.

THE SECRET ROOM

If someone is on the run and lying low in your castle, keep them well-hidden in your secret room with a hidden revolving door.

WHAT YOU NEED

- Strong corrugated card
- Paper
- Scissors and a craft knife
- Felt-tip pens
- Strong glue or a glue gun
- A wooden skewer or cocktail stick
- Small cardboard boxes
- White tissues
- Cotton wool pads or balls
- Scraps of fabric

1 Measure the width and height of your bedchamber and cut a piece of corrugated card the same size to make a wall. Make sure the lines in the corrugated cardboard run up and down, so that when you look at the top of the wall, you can see a row of little holes.

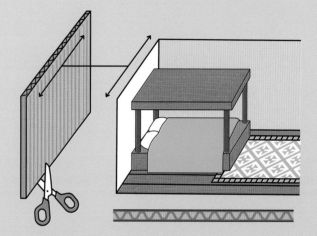

2 Use felt-tips to draw shelves full of books on the wall.

3 Draw a small door shape on the wall with the bottom a little way up from the floor. Use a ruler to make sure it is a perfect rectangle. Carefully cut out the door, leaving a neat hole in the wall.

4 On the back of the door, draw the same pattern of books as on the front.

5 Fit the door back into the hole in the wall. Push the pointy end of the skewer up through the cardboard in the base of the wall and up through the middle of the door. At the top of the door, push through into the wall.

6 Cut off the skewer or cocktail stick level with the bottom of the wall. You should now be able to swivel the door around to open and close it. When it's closed, it will blend in with the bookshelves.

7 Fit the wall into one end of the bedchamber, leaving a small space behind it. Use some glue to hold it in place. If you like, you can also make a small bed, close-stool (see pages 18–19) and other furniture and objects for the secret room.

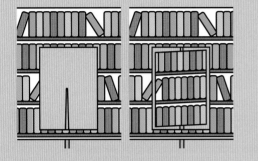

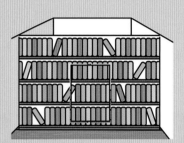

THE HISTORY BIT!

In 1745 Alexander Irvine, the Laird (or Lord) of Drum Castle in Scotland, fought for the Scottish Jacobites against the English in the famous Battle of Culloden. The Jacobites lost and Alexander fled for his life. His sister Mary kept him hidden in a secret room at Drum Castle for three years to avoid capture by the English.

THE TILT YARD

To practise their skills and provide entertainment, medieval knights took part in jousting contests. Two knights would charge towards each other and each tried to knock the other off his horse, using a long lance. This took place on a special jousting ground called a tilt yard.

1 Using a ruler and pencil, draw a rectangle about 12 cm wide and 45 cm long on the corrugated card. Cut it out. Cut a long strip of corrugated card, the same length as your rectangle and about 1 cm wide.

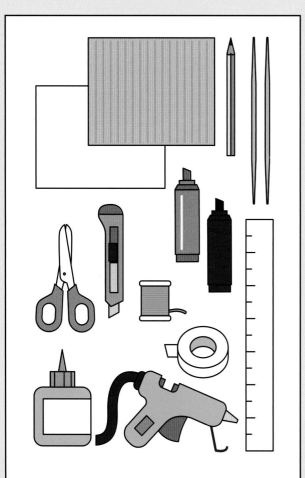

2 Cut about 40 3-cm-long pieces of skewer or cocktail stick. Draw a line down the middle of the large cardboard rectangle. Use a skewer or cocktail stick to make a row of holes along the line about 1 cm apart.

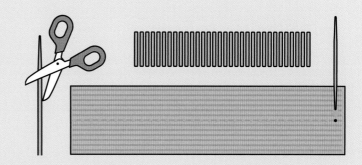

3 Stick the pieces of skewer or cocktail stick into the holes and secure them with glue. Take the long strip of cardboard and fit it on top of the row of sticks, pushing them in between the layers of cardboard. Add some glue if you need to.

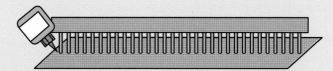

WHAT YOU NEED

- Strong corrugated card
- A ruler and a pencil
- Wooden skewers or cocktail sticks
- Strong glue or a glue gun
- Sticky tape (invisible if possible)
- Smooth card
- Scissors and a craft knife
- Felt-tip or marker pens
- Strong sewing thread

4 On the smooth card, draw two knights on horseback about 7 cm long. You could copy or trace a picture from a book or from the Internet, or copy the knights on this page. Carefully cut the knights out and colour them in with felt-tip pens.

5 Cut two door-shaped pieces of corrugated cardboard about 2 cm wide and 7 cm long. Cut two pieces of skewer or cocktail stick about 5 cm long. Stick the pointed ends at a right angle into the middle of the pieces of cardboard.

6 Use glue or sticky tape to attach the knights to the sticks. Take two longer pieces of skewer and fix them to the knights to act as lances.

7 Use a skewer or cocktail stick to make a small hole in the front of each door-shaped piece of card. Tie a piece of thread about 50 cm long into each one.

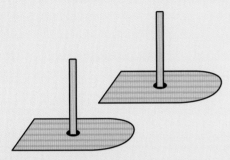

8 You can now line up the knights on either side of the tilt yard, and pull the strings to make them charge towards each other.

TIP
If the knights don't stand up easily, they may need wider bases.

TAKE IT FURTHER ...
Can you build stands for the audience to sit on to watch the jousting?

TIP
Give the knights different coloured horse blankets and helmet plumes, so the audience can tell them apart!

MANGONEL ATTACK!

If enemies decide to besiege your castle, they'll probably bring their mangonel. This is a type of giant catapult used to shoot rocks at castles to smash down their walls. Yikes!

WHAT YOU NEED

- 30 wooden lolly sticks or craft sticks
- Strong glue or a glue gun
- Thin string or strong sewing thread
- A strong elastic band
- A small or narrow cardboard box
- Newspaper or scrap paper
- Paint and paintbrushes (optional)

If your wooden sticks and string are a natural colour, you don't need to paint them – they'll look realistic as they are.

1 Glue two sticks together so that they overlap in the middle. Repeat with another two sticks. As the mangonel has to be very strong, you also need to wrap string or thread around the joins several times and tie it tightly.

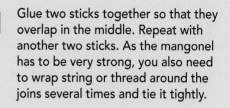

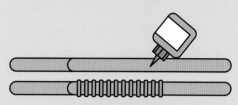

2 Glue two more sticks to each piece, overlapping slightly at the top, to make triangle shapes. Before joining up the last corner, thread one strong elastic band onto both triangles. When the glue is dry, use more string or thread to wrap around and strengthen the joins.

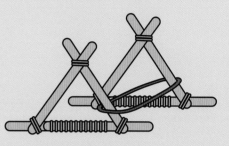

3 Glue about 20 sticks together in a block to make a strong base for your mangonel. Line up the triangle shaped pieces on each side of the base, and glue them on, too. Strengthen the structure by wrapping and tying more string or thread around it.

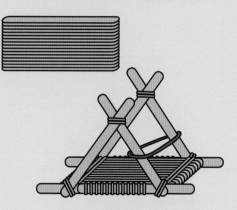

4 Cut or break a lolly stick to fit across the top of the two triangles. Use string to tie both ends on tightly. At this point, if you want to, you can paint the mangonel and leave it to dry.

5 Twist the middle of the elastic band around a few times, then push a lolly stick into the middle of it.

6 Position the stick so that one end of it is held by the elastic band and the rest reaches through the mangonel frame, between the triangles. The elastic should make it spring up against the top bar. (If it doesn't, try twisting the elastic band the other way.)

7 Cut a tray shape from the end of your small cardboard box and glue it to the top of the long end of the stick. You can now place a missile in the tray, pull the stick down, and release it to fire the missile.

8 To make realistic rocks, scrunch up balls of newspaper or scrap paper, make them an uneven shape, and paint them grey. You can use some glue to make sure the paper stays scrunched up.

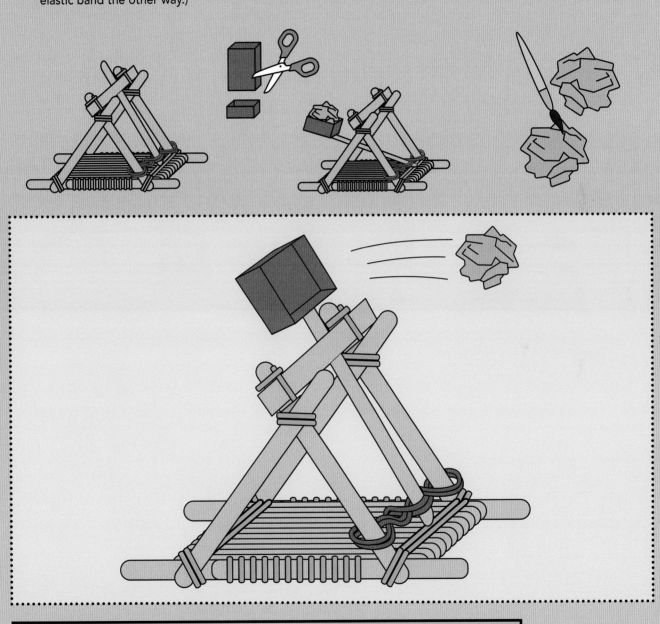

THE HISTORY BIT!

As well as rocks, attackers sometimes used a mangonel to fling dead animals over the walls to spread disease, or bundles of burning rags to try to start a fire.

THE GROUNDS AND MOAT

Some castles stand alone, but most have large enclosed grounds around them, sometimes with a moat and more buildings too. Your tilt yard can go here as well.

WHAT YOU NEED

- A very large piece of cardboard
- Thick card
- Scissors and a craft knife
- Felt-tip or marker pens
- Paints and paintbrushes
- Strong glue or a glue gun
- Clear acetate or clear plastic food bags
- Smaller cardboard boxes and tubes
- Green paper or white glitter
- Small dry twigs with several branches
- Modelling clay
- Felt or fabric (optional)
- Sand and small pebbles (optional)

You can get a really big piece of cardboard from the box of a large appliance, such as a washing machine. If you can't find one, tape several smaller pieces of cardboard together.

1 First, cut your cardboard into the shape you want. It could be a square, oval, hexagon or whatever you like, but make sure you keep it as large as possible. Carefully pick up your castle and position it in the middle.

2 Use strips of thick cardboard, about 7–10 cm wide, to make a low outer wall around the grounds. Fold over about 1 cm at the base of each piece of wall, to glue them to the edge of your grounds. Leave an open gateway facing the front door of the castle.

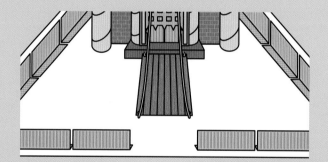

3 Use a marker or felt-tip to draw a moat around the castle, making sure it is narrow enough for the drawbridge to cross it. Add a path from the gateway up to the drawbridge. You could also use small narrow cardboard boxes or tubes to make gateposts.

4 Paint the pathway a stony colour and the rest of the grounds a grassy green. If you have green felt or fabric, you could use that to make the grass instead. You could also cover the pathway with glue, sprinkle it with sand, and arrange pebbles along the sides.

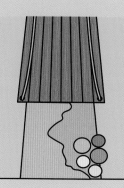

5 Paint the moat a watery blue or blue-green colour. When the paint is dry, cover it with a layer of clear acetate or clear plastic cut from food bags. You can also add pebbles along the edges of the moat.

6 Make trees using small branching twigs stuck into pieces of brown modelling clay to help them stand up. Make little leaves from paper and glue them on – or for a wintery scene, put some glue along the tops of the branches and sprinkle them with white glitter.

7 A dovecot is a nesting house for pigeons, which were then put into pies! Make one using a round box or tube. Make a flat roof from a circle of card, with a hole in the middle so the pigeons can fly in and out. Decorate it to look like it's made of stone and add a little door.

TIP
Keep your castle in a safe place and don't leave it where anyone could trip over it!

TAKE IT FURTHER ...
If you want to add even more things to your castle, what about a stable for the knights' horses, a walled rose garden, or strings of tiny paper bunting?

AND HERE IS YOUR FINISHED CASTLE!

GLOSSARY

Acetate Thin, clear, stiff plastic used in packaging, or available at hobby stores.

Arrow slits Tall, narrow castle windows that arrows can be fired out of.

Battlements Walls around the top of a castle with regular spaces in them.

Beseige To surround and attack a castle.

Bradawl A sharp, pointed tool for making neat holes.

Coat of arms A shield-shaped picture or design used to represent a family, town or organisation.

Dovecot A building for pigeons to shelter and nest in.

Drawbridge A bridge over a castle moat, which can be raised to prevent enemies crossing the moat.

Gatehouse A strong building surrounding the entrance to a castle.

Glue gun A gun-shaped electric tool that heats up and applies strong glue.

Goblet An old-fashioned, bowl-shaped drinking cup with a stem.

Jacobites Supporters of the Stuart royal family of King James II of England, who wanted the Stuarts to rule England and Scotland.

Jousting A sport in which two knights tried to knock each other off their horses using lances.

Knight An armed soldier who rode a horse and served a lord or king.

Lance A long wooden spear with a pointed steel tip.

Mangonel A machine used to fire rocks and other large missiles at a castle.

Medieval Dating from the Middle Ages in Europe, the period from around 500 to 1500 CE.

Moat A deep, wide, water-filled ditch surrounding a castle to keep enemies out.

Plume A bunch of long feathers worn on top of a helmet.

Portcullis A strong metal gate that can be lowered down over a doorway to block it.

Tapestry A thick cloth with threads sewn or woven into it to make patterns or pictures.

Tilt yard An area for holding jousting contests.

Turret A small tower at the corner of a building or wall, or on top of a larger tower.

Wood panelling Sheets of wood used to cover a wall.

FURTHER INFORMATION

WHERE TO GET MATERIALS

Everyday items
You'll probably have some everyday items and craft materials at home already, such as foil, food wrap, pens, tissues, string, paper and card, sticky tape, glue and scissors.

Recycling
Old packaging that's going to be thrown away or recycled is a great source of making materials, such as cardboard boxes, yoghurt pots, ice cream tubs, cardboard tubes, magazines, old wrapping paper and newspaper.

Supermarkets
Great for basic items you might not have at home, such as paper cups, cotton wool, a sewing kit, paper straws, wooden skewers and battery-powered fairy lights.

Outdoors
Collect things like leaves, twigs, acorns and seashells for free!

Specialist shops
Hobby and craft shops, sewing shops, art shops, garden centres and DIY stores could be useful for things like a craft knife and a glue gun, acetate, modelling clay, fabric, sand and pebbles. If you don't have the shop you need near you, ask an adult to help you look for online shops, such as Hobbycraft.

Charity shops
It's always a good idea to check charity shops when you can, as they often have all kinds of handy household items and craft materials at very low prices.

BOOKS

The Usborne Book of Castles by Lesley Sims, Usborne, 2015

Stephen Biesty's Cross-Sections: Castle by Stephen Biesty, DK, 2019

Everything Castles by Crispin Boyer, National Geographic, 2011

Dark Knights and Dingy Castles by Terry Deary, Scholastic, 2017

Junk Modelling by Annalees Lim, Wayland, 2016

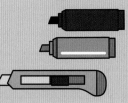

WEBSITES

PBS Design Squad
https://pbskids.org/designsquad/
Lots of brilliant design and build challenges

DIY
https://diy.org/
An online maker community for kids

Parents.com Arts & Crafts
https://www.parents.com/fun/arts-crafts/?page=1
Maker projects, instructions and videos

Kiwico DIY page
https://www.kiwico.com/diy/
Fun and easy maker ideas

INDEX

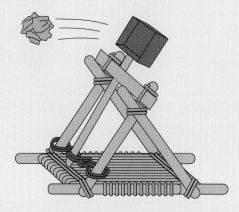

MAKER MODELS

SERIES CONTENT LIST

On the move! • Elastic band car • Paddle boat • Cable car • Propeller plane • Going up! • Helicopter • Jetpack • Maglev train • Multi-mode transport interchange • And here s your finished transport hub! • Glossary and further information • Index

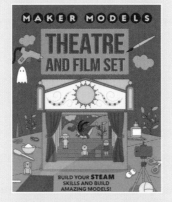

The stage is yours! • Theatre and stage • The swish of the curtain! • In the spotlight • Set design • Stars of the stage • Fly system • Gone in a puff of smoke • Pepper's ghost • Cinema projector • Stop-motion movie • Theatre house • And here's is your finished theatre! • Glossary and further information • Index

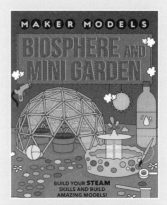

Grow a garden! • Garden base • Grass art • Bean tree • Wildflower corner • Geodesic dome greenhouse • Greenhouse garden • Fountain • Summer house • The finished garden • And here's is your finished biosphere and mini-garden! • Glossary and further information • Index

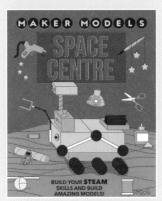

Reach for the stars! • We have lift-off! • Launch pad • Command module • Parachute descent • Space satellite • Human gyroscope • Passenger spaceship • Mars rover • Planetarium projector • Space centre • And here is your finished space centre! • Glossary and further information • Index

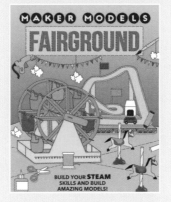

All the fun of the fair • Helter skelter • Chair swing ride • Fairground stalls • Big wheel • Dodgems • Carousel • Rollercoaster • The fairground • Here is your finished fairground! • Glossary and further information • Index

Holding the fort • Castle walls and battlements • Towers and turrets • The grand gatehouse • Door and portcullis • Raise the drawbridge! • The great hall • The bedchamber • The secret room • The tilt yard • Mangonel attack! • The grounds and moat • And here is your fi nished castle!• Glossary and further information • Index